Visual Manna's

Teaching Math

Through Art

by

Sharon Jeffus

This book is dedicated to Angie Gray. It exists because of her help and wisdom.

Copyright 2008

Introduction

Math can be a very difficult subject for artistically inclined students. This text is a supplement to a math textbook. The approach here is different. The goal is that students can see the connection between art and cooking, architecture, engineering and things in everyday life! Math was always very difficult for me, primarily because I wanted to see everything in a visual way. Fractions, understanding angles, two and three dimensional objects and other mathmatical concepts are presented here in a visual and kinesthetic manner. Master artists have used mathmatical principals for centuries. Recognizing and counting money and telling time are important math skills.

This book shows geometric and spatial sense involving measurement (including length, area, volume), and similarity and transformations of shapes.

This book also shows mathematical systems (including real numbers, whole numbers, integers, fractions), geometry, and number theory (including primes, factors, multiples). Most important, it is a different approach to the study of math! It can be appropriate for children grades three through eight and lessons can be modified for different ages.

Table of Contents

Research has been done that shows that children learn more by doing and seeing, than just by filling in workbook pages. Go to this website for information on Dale's Cone of Learning:
http://www.cals.ncsu.edu/agexed/sae/ppt1/sld012.htm
The fractal below was created by Bert Hickman.

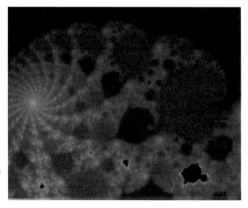

The picture below was done by the master Renaissance artist Raphael called "School of Athens." It is a mathmatical wonder. The formation of the groupings and use of perspective is profound. Go to this website:
:http://www.mcm.edu/academic/galileo/ars/arshtml/arch5.html and read about the connection. From ancient art to modern day fractals, math and art are seen in combination with each other.

Even the microwaved DVD on the left is considered a fractal. Even the fractal art below is considered math and art and called "Bubbles."

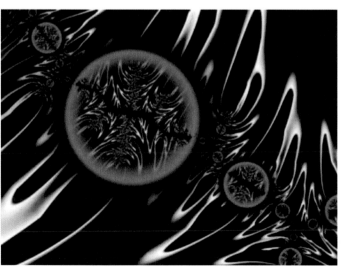

Clocks are truly works of art. Clocks can be part of architecture, as in England's famous "Big Ben." They also can be a part of fashion as in a wrist watch. They can be a part of sports when a stop watch is used. Clocks can be analog or digital. Telling and measuring time is an important skill in math.

KREWE OF NEREVS
GRAND OPERA HOUSE
FEBRUARY THE 21st 1900.
1900

One of my student's favorite projects is designing a colorwheel clock. We did a "It's time to say I love you clock." Each student made a clock with the time that they say "I love you" to someone in their family. A good idea is an "It's time for breakfast colorwheel clock." They can make breakfast items around the clock, or even design a clock in the shape of an egg. Lunch can be a hamburger colorwheel clock. The dials can be french fries. It can be fun and very creative when students begin to start telling time on an analogue clock. Make sure their time is correct and that you count hour, minutes and seconds with them. You can even use a brad and cut out the clock hands and make them move.

Directions:
Cut out and color the colorwheel below. Glue this on a piece of paper. Allow students to design a clock and use the colorwheel as the face of the clock.

The picture above is by Diego Valaquez and shows a clock worn in the mid 1600's.

Just for fun go to yard sales and see if you can find any very inexpensive analog clocks. Give children a screwdriver and see if they can take them apart and fix them if they are broken. We did this when my sons were young!

Time

Telling time is a very important skill. Sometimes we get very used to digital clocks, and don't learn how to use analog clocks. This is a mathmatical skill. An analog clock has a face with the two/three hands. The face of the clock gets divided in two hands. The first hand points to hours. It is marked with the hours going from 1 to 12. The second division is the minutes, the other hand marks minutes. Every hour has 60 minutes and every minute has 60 seconds. For every hour mark, there are five minutes of the minute hand. What time does the clock below say? Go to this website for more lessons on telling time: http://www.arcytech.org/java/clock/.

Make clock faces and draw the hands to show the times given:

1:00

5:15   8:30   3:45

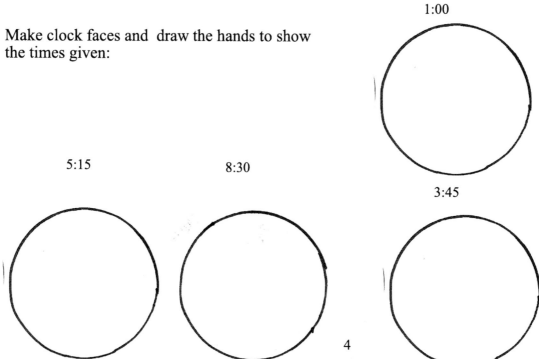

Aside from telling time, it is important to know how to tell the difference in time.
Problem:
1. The Browns left on vacation at 8:16 am to go to Yellowstone Park. They arrived at 10:37 am. How long did it take for them to get there? To find the difference in time, you treat it like subtraction, lining up the columns.

2. Josie was asked to babysit for her neighbors. They left at 6:49 pm and returned at 11:35 pm. How long did she babysit?

A project suggestion is to have students design a clock. The clock below is Big Ben in London, England. The hour hand is nine feet long. The minute hand is fourteen feet long. What time is it on the clock? Go to this website to see the whole clock and read about it: http://en.wikipedia.org/wiki/Big_Ben.
"Melting Watches," by Salvadore Dali has analogue
watches on it that are melting. Go to this website to see the picture:
http://upload.wikimedia.org/wikipedia/en/d/dd/The_Persistence_of_Memory.jpg
Have children design a building with a clock face on it somewhere. Have them count out the minutes when they put the time on it. An architect is someone who designs art that you can walk through. It requires math skills to design buildings.

Fractions:

Fractions are a way of expressing a part of a whole amount. For a fraction you have a top and bottom number. On the top is the part called the numerator. It can be any number. On the bottom is the entire number, called the denominator. It can be any number except zero. It does not make sense to have a group of zeros or a whole of zero.

numerator = part

denominator = whole

Use the picture given to explore fractions. How many note papers are there? ____ If you said 12 you are right! That is the whole number. It appears on the bottom. It is the denominator. How many yellow notepads are there? That is the part. That goes on top. It is the numerator.

The fraction is: 2/12.

Color the notes. What would be the fraction for the blue notes?

Can you figure the fraction for the yellow and blue notes together?

yellow + blue

2/12 +4/12 = 6/12 or 1/2.

Make up your own fraction problem.

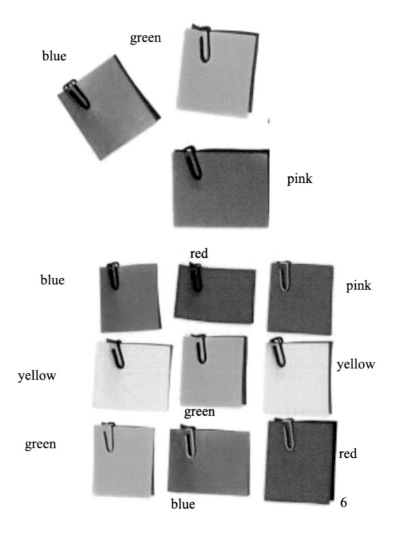

Purchase a Hersey's milk chocolate candy bar. Break the bar into two pieces. Each piece is one half of the whole. Break the two pieces into two. Now you have fourths. When you break the fourths into half, you have eighths. Each part is a fraction of the whole candy bar. Go ahead and enjoy your math problem by eating the chocolate!

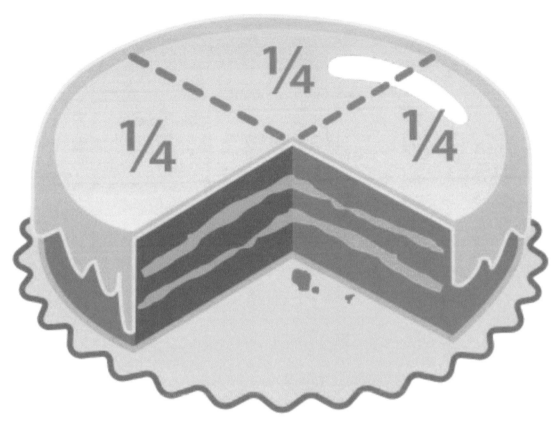

This cake is divided into fourths. Can you imagine eating a piece of cake that is one fourth of the whole cake? It is hard to imagine. Draw a cake and divide it into eight parts. Each part would be 1/8 of a whole. All together there are eight parts. The recipe below is for a cake. Bake this cake and then cut it into 8 parts. Fractions are even important for cooking!!!! Now double this recipe to make a cake twice as large. Choose any cake recipe you want to do this project, or use the one below.

Divide the pie above into two parts. Each part is 1/2. Divide the pieces into two parts. Each part is 1/4. Divide the fourth pieces into two parts. Each part is 1/8 of a pie. Do you think you could eat 1/8 of a pie? How about 1/4 of a pie? If you can get a pie and really do this, it would be a wonderful addition to the lesson.

Angel Food Cake
12 egg whites
1 1/2 teaspoons tartar
3/4 cup granulated sugar
1 1/2 teaspoons pure vanilla extract
1/2 teaspoon almond extract
1 cup sifted cake flour
1 1/4 cups confectioner's sugar
1/4 teaspoon salt
Beat egg whites and tartar until foamy
Add sugar, beating constantly.
Beat in vanilla and almond.
Sift flour, salt and sugar together.
Put in pan and bake at 350 degrees for 30 to 40 minutes.

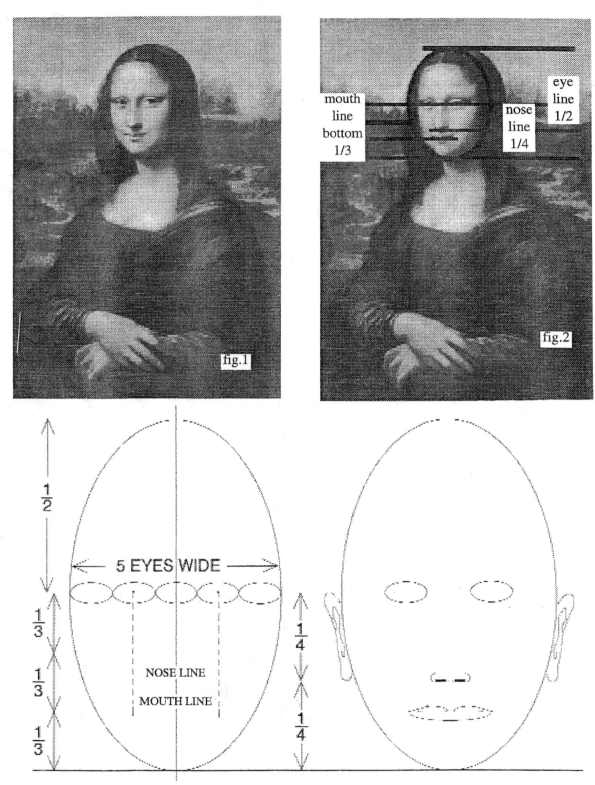

fig.1

mouth line bottom 1/3

nose line 1/4

eye line 1/2

fig.2

$\frac{1}{2}$

5 EYES WIDE

$\frac{1}{3}$

$\frac{1}{3}$

$\frac{1}{3}$

NOSE LINE

MOUTH LINE

$\frac{1}{4}$

$\frac{1}{4}$

Above are examples of using the classic Greek proportions of the face. You can see the fractions used in the master work of art the "Mona Lisa." Draw the Mona Lisa using correct proportions.

8

Fractions found in drawing the face:

You use fractions when you draw a face using the Classic Greek proportions of the face. The pictures on this page were put into fractions by the master artist Leonardo da Vinci. The eye line divides the face in half. When you divide the eye line to the chin line in half again, you have the place to put the bottom of the nose.

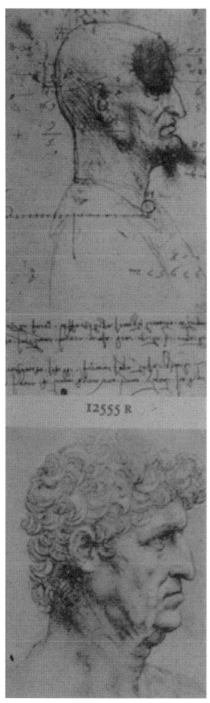

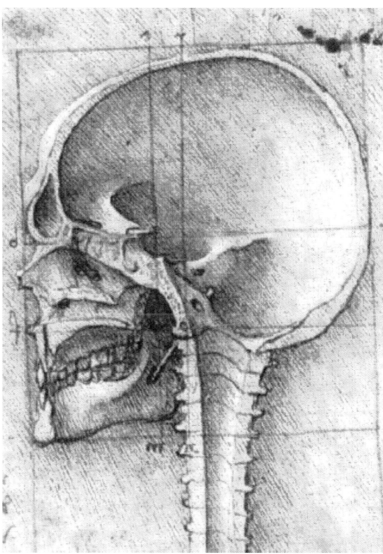

9

DRAWING THE FACE IN PROPORTION

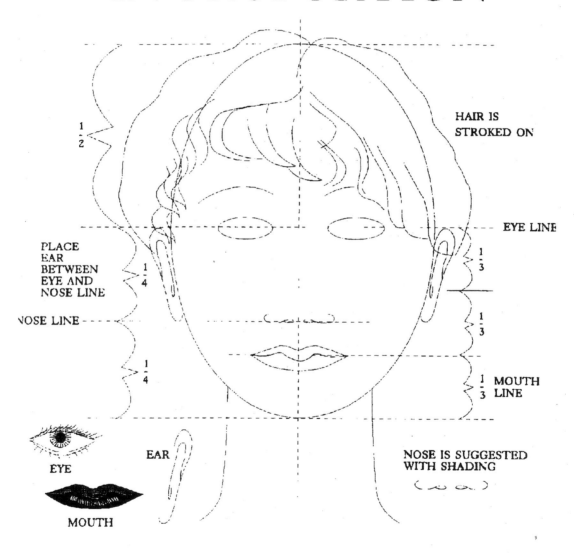

HAIR IS STROKED ON

$\frac{1}{2}$

EYE LINE

PLACE EAR BETWEEN EYE AND NOSE LINE

$\frac{1}{3}$

$\frac{1}{4}$

$\frac{1}{3}$

NOSE LINE

$\frac{1}{4}$

$\frac{1}{3}$ MOUTH LINE

NOSE IS SUGGESTED WITH SHADING

EYE

EAR

MOUTH

Look in the mirror and draw a self
portrait using the fractions above.

Triptyche:

We are going to design a work of art using fractions. A triptych is a panel painting that is divided into three pieces. The middle part is usually larger. The two side parts can usually be folded across the middle picture and carried from place to place with the idea that in medieval times, altar pieces were carried from one place of worship to another. Look at the triptychs below. What basic shapes do you see? Design a triptych. A polyptych refers to a painting which is divided into four or more sections, or panels. The term diptych is used to describe a two-part painting. The terms tetraptych (4 parts), pentaptych (5), hexaptych (6), heptaptych (7), and octaptych (8) are also sometimes used.

The triptych above left is in three parts. How many parts do you see in the work of art above right? It is the master work "The Isenheim Altarpiece" by Matthias Grunewald. Each part is one fourth of the whole design.

Design your own tryptyche. Make sure the middle section is twice as large as the two sides. 11

Sequences:

Sequences are finding a pattern in a listing of numbers. Once a pattern is found, you can write a mathmatical sentence, called an equation. This equation allows you to predict any future values.

The best way to start finding your sequence is to use a chart to look at the pattern you have been given. So, for the picture we have below, we are given five sets of balls stacked in a triangle. We can count the balls in each set and see how many balls we have added each time to see if that makes a pattern.

Ball pattern	total balls	pattern
A	1	0
B	3	2
C	6	3
D	10	4
E	15	5
F		
G		
H		

The pattern is adding the number of balls you have and the number of the sequence. For instance, for D, you had 6 balls for C and added 4 because D was 4th in the sequence.

Complete the cart to H, and figure out how many balls there would be. You should get 36 as your final answer.

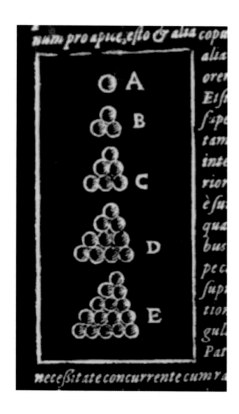

The creator of the picture on the left was Johannes Kepler, a famous mathmetician and astronomer of the 17th century. An astronomer is someone who studies the stars. This picture was from his "A New Year's Gift of Hexagonal Snow". In this paper, he investigated the hexagonal symmetry of snowflakes and he made a statement about the most efficient arrangement for packing spheres.

Cubes are fun to draw. See the figure below. When you look at a cube, you can see three sides. When you draw your cubes, make sure you make them look three dimensional by showing 3 sides. Complete the pattern to F.   See if you get the same sequence. Can you copy the Kepler pattern?

Number of Cubes   Cubes Added

A.

B.

C.

D.

E.

F.

Describe the Sequence:

Draw a pattern that has a different sequence:

Describe the sequence:

When you draw your cube, make sure you color it in the primary colors. Primary colors are red, yellow and blue.

A cube is a regular solid having six congruent square faces.

There is a very famous mechanical puzzle invented in 1974 by the Hungarian sculptor and professor of architecture Ernő Rubik called the Rubik's Cube. It is said to be the world's best-selling toy, with some 300,000,000 Rubik's Cubes and imitations sold worldwide. Rubik probably had to learn about sequencing to invent the cube. Can you think of a toy that uses sequencing in a similar way?   13

What is the picture on this page an example of?

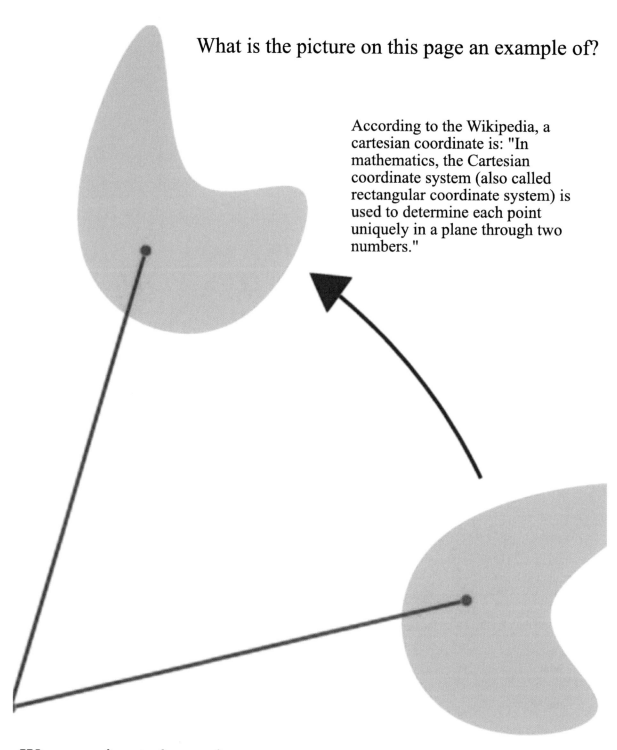

According to the Wikipedia, a cartesian coordinate is: "In mathematics, the Cartesian coordinate system (also called rectangular coordinate system) is used to determine each point uniquely in a plane through two numbers."

We are going to learn about:

Reflection: flips image over axis of cartesian coordinate/ looks like a mirror image. Shape does not change.

Translation: image is moved from place to place on coordinate system. shape does not change, will look the same in both places.

Rotation: image or object is rotated around center point, rotational symmetry is where the image or object looks the same as the original placement.

Reflections

Objective:
-To understand what an object looks like when it has been reflected.
-How to reflect an object over an x- or y- axis of a cartesian coordinate system.

Notice the beautiful reflection of the Taj Mahal in the water in front of it. You can even see how the sky is reflected. It looks as if the water is a mirror. We do a similar thing when we create a reflection over the cartesian coordinate system. The cartesian coordinate system is made up of a x-axis going horizontally, a y-axis going vertically, and an origin where the two axis meet. The two axis are then numbered to locate points along the axis going horizontally and vertically. An example:

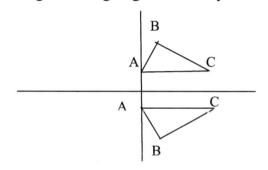

The x-axis is the horizontal, or across, line.
The y-axis is the vertical, or up-and-down line.
ABC is the original object.
A'B'C' is the reflection, reflected below the x axis.

The Taj Majal, completed around 1682, is a mausoleum located in Agra, India. It was built under Mughal Emperor Shah Jahan in memory of his favorite wife, Mumtaz Mahal. It is considered the finest example of Mughal architecture, a style that combines elements from Persian, Turkish, Indian, and Islamic architectural styles. It is one of the most famous buildings in human history. Also famous is the way you can see the reflection in the water.

15

Reflection in Art

One of the most famous examples of reflection in art history is this painting by the master Renaissance artist Caraveggio. He painted Narcisus who saw his reflection in the water and fell in love with himself. When someone loves themselves and is proud, they are called narcistic.

ʌibɘqiʞiw | wikipediʌ

Leonardo da Vinci's writing was famous as being backwards. It is as though he looked into a mirror and wrote backwards. A reflection is a mirror image. Write your name on a piece of paper. Hold it in front of a mirror. What happens?

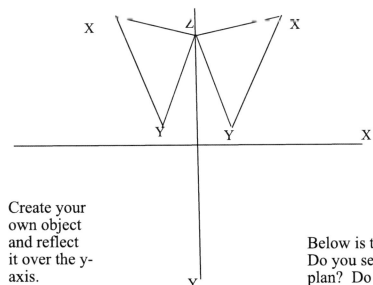

xyz is the original

x'y'z' is the reflection, reflected over the y-axis

Create your own object and reflect it over the y-axis.

Below is the floor plan of the Taj Mahal. Do you see the reflection in the floor plan? Do you see symmetry?

Do you see the reflection in the picture below? How does it change what you see?

Translations

Objectives:
- To be able to identify a translation.
- How to create a translation over a translation on a cartesian coordinate system.

Translations are closely related to reflections. Translations are on the move in a different way.

Notice how a ball is moving across a page; an object being translated is going to be moved across the caresian coordinate system. When you translate an object, you will be moving a specified number of spaces horizontally and or vertically. Or, said another way, along the y- and or x-axis. Go to this website to see an animation of this: http://www.mathsisfun.com/geometry/translation.html. When you make your flip book, make a ball and move it 1/16 of an inch on every page. When you flip your book, it will look like it is moving.

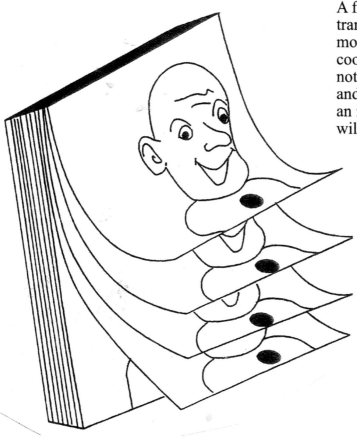

A flipbook is a way of doing a translation. A translation image moves from place to place on a coordinate system. The shape does not change. You can take this head and move it across the page 1/16 of an inch at a time in a flip book. It will look like it is moving.

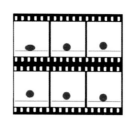

Go to this website to see many different animations. A fipbook is a primitive example of an animation:
http://commons.wikimedia.org/wiki/Category:Animations

For translations, notice the shape stays the same. For reflections, the shape flips, it becomes the opposite. Go to this website:
http://en.wikipedia.org/wiki/Image:Galilean_transform_of_world_line.gif

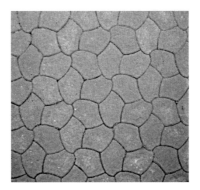

Notice the pattern above. See how it is translated to be repeated to make the sidewalk. Practice making a translation by continuing the pattern on the picture above.

Money

Objectives:
To count money when given an amount to find
To find change
In American money, it is divided into coins and paper money.

Visual recognition of coins is very important in learning how to count money and find change.
Name the money amounts below.

Do you know the name of the person on the twenty dollar bill?

Paper dollars include the:
one dollar bill
five dollar bill
ten dollar bill
twenty dollar bill
fifty dollar bill
one-hundred dollar bill
five-hundred dollar bill
one-thousand dollar bill

Go to this website to see a painting by Harnett. He painted paper money so realistically that in 1886 he got arrested for counterfeiting:
http://www.nga.gov/feature/artnation/harnett/money_1.shtm

Different amount bills have different portraits on them. Go to this website to see what the different bills look like:http://en.wikipedia.org/wiki/Federal_Reserve_Note

Given the amount of money, tell me how you could make the money with coins and dollars (if needed). Sometimes there is more than one way to make the sum:

Example: $3.65   3 one dollar bills   or   2 one dollar bills
                           2 quarters   4 quarters
                           1 dime   6 dimes
                           1 nickel   1 nickel   What other combinations?

Both ways add up to make $3.65. There are actually more ways. Can you find them? Here are some problems for you. These might be easier for you if you can use some change. Try to find as many ways as you can to make the following amounts:

1. $.67
2. $2.83
3. $7.36
4. $4.31
5. $16.46

Another important skill to know is how to make change. Many times when you pay for something at the store, you may not pay for it exactly. Therefore, you need to know how much you should receive back from the cashier. Or, if you are selling something and they give you too much, you need to figure out how much change to give them. Many times we want to only rely on calculators and computers, but it is very important to know this on your own. Machines are not always right. If you do not know how to do this, you will not know if you are getting or giving the right change. Plus, if you do not have a calculator/computer nearby, you can do the math on your own.

Let's examine how we can do this. I'm at the grocery store. I had to get some bread for $1.59, milk for $2.29 and oranges for $.75. Together with the tax it totalled $5.96. I paid with a ten dollar bill. How much change should the cashier give me? Remember to line up your decimal points when adding or subtracting.

$$\begin{array}{r} \$10.00 \\ \underline{-5.96} \end{array}$$

Do these problems. If you have the money and can count amounts out, that would be great:
1. You are purchasing a CD for $13.88, plus a tax of $1.03, equalling $14.91. You're paying with a $20.00 bill. What is your change?

2. You're taking a couple of friends for pizza. You get a large pizza for $12.99, 3 salad bars for $5.97, 3 large sodas for $5.97. The total with taxes and tip comes to $26.93. You pay with a twenty dollar bill and two five dollar bills, what should your change be?

3. You decide to decorate your room. You buy: 2 posters costing $7.00; a bulletin board for $8.95, a gallon of paint for $17.95 and a set of candles for $10.00. The total with tax is $46.30. You pay with 2 twenty and 1 ten dollar bill. What should your change be?

4. You decided to upgrade your mountain bike so you are selling yours. You advertise your bike for $135. When you sell it the customer gives you 2 fifties, 1 twenty, and 2 ten dollar bills. How much change do you give him?

On the left are the dollar bills that we use frequently. Write the name of the famous person on the front of each bill below the bill.

Be Creative: Foreign money

Every country has their own currency. Find the name and design for the currency for at least three other countries. What is the currency for Europe? European currency is worth different amounts from American currency. Draw and color the currency of the countries you have found. Did you know that the United States is the only country that does not have currency in color?

When you visit a foreign country, you trade your American dollars for the dollars for that country. It is based on a mathematical formula. It is also based on how well America is doing economically. If America is doing well economically, you can buy more in the country you are visiting. On the other hand, if America is not doing well, you will not be able to spend much on your visit. Pretend you have your own country. Name your country and then design currency for it.

One way that children can remember who is on
each bill is to draw a picture and do a study of
the person. We can start with the one dollar bill.

 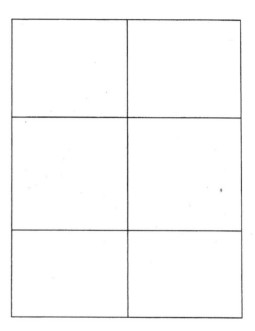

Draw your one dollar bill in the space below.

Measuring Angles

Objective:
Measuring Angles with a Protractor to fit a Pattern
Degrees of a Circle

A protractor will be needed for this lesson
You can print your own protractor at: http://www.ossmann.com/protractor/ and to
see how to use a protractor in animation go to:
http://www.mathopenref.com/constmeasureangle.html

To use the protractor you need to start by putting the center point of the protractor
on the center point of the design. Then place the zero degrees on one of the lines.
Then go to the next line and measure that angle on the protractor. What is that
angle?

Keep your protractor the same place and keep measuring the angles until you get to
the straight angle or 180 degrees. List your angles beside the design.

Now do the same thing with the protractor turned the exact opposite.

What is the difference in each angle? If not exact everytime, what is the
approximation? How many angles are there? Multiply the number of angles by the
measure of the angles. You should have gotten something like 360 degrees. Three
hundred sixty degrees is the number of degrees in a circle.

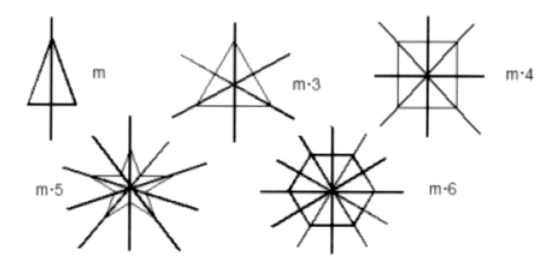

Angles (2)

Following the same directions for the prior exercise, we will find the angles for the photo at the bottom. Place the center point of your protractor with the center point of the photograph. Line up the straight edge to what would be the middle of the reinforcement. Measure to the middle. What is that measure? Again, go around until you get to the straight angle, or 180 degrees. Record your angles.

Angle 1=
Angle 2=
Angle 3=

Now, flip your protractor over and do the same thing over again.

Angle 1=
Angle 2=
Angle 3=

What was the difference between the angles? How many angles are there? Multiply the two amounts together? You should get something like 360 degrees. Remember, the degrees of a circle are 360 degrees.

Independent practice: Given is a picture of a snowflake. Follow the directions for the two problems worked together and find the angles of the snowflake. Also find the sum of the angles to see what your total degrees measure for the angles is (should be the same as a circle.

Radial lines are lines that come out from the center.

Project idea:
Use tempera paint and paint the angle lines above. While the paint is wet, fold the paper over and over until you can barely see the original lines. Let this dry and create an abstract design.

Radial Symmetry

Objectives:
- Create a radial design using angle measurement.
- Find lines of symmetry.

Materials needed:
    12" x 12" white paper
    colored pencils or markers
    protractor

The design you are creating will have radial symmetry. Or, easily said, symmetry of particular circular objects. This means that there will be symmetry where something can be divided into identical halves by a line passing through a central point at any angle.

Directions:

1) Find the center point of the paper. This can easily be done by folding the paper carefully into fourths. Where the folds meet, you will have the center point.

2) Draw a line segment along one of the folds, and through the center point.

3) Place your protractor with the centerpoint at the center of the paper and along the segment you drew.

4) Begin marking your paper at 30 degree increments at about 2" away from the center point. Measure until you get to the straight angle, or 180 degrees.

5) Turn your protractor around and do the same thing going the other way around. When you do all of this, that will be the total degrees of the circle? It will be 360 degrees. That is the total measure of degrees for any circle.

6) Using the degree markings, draw a similar curved shape radiating from the center point. Make it interesting, but not too complicated or your project will become too difficult.

7) For alternating spaces you will be doing some lettering. For two of the spaces you can use your name. For the other four think of things that describe you. It may be a characteristic, something you do, something you're good at, or something you think of on your own. When you are done with your lettering, you can color those in with your favorite color.

8) For the other sections, choose colors to radiate away from the center point. You may want to use the color wheel. As a reminder, that would be: red, orange, yellow, green, blue and violet.

Now, returning to radial symmetry. If you draw your designs from your center point evenly it wil be easier to see. If you draw a line going through the center point of your design, do you have the same thing on the other side? How many lines can you find that will do this? Any line that you try should do this. The lines of symmetry are what we call infinite. That means they go on forever, we cannot begin to count that high.

Can you tell what you learned about in this lesson?

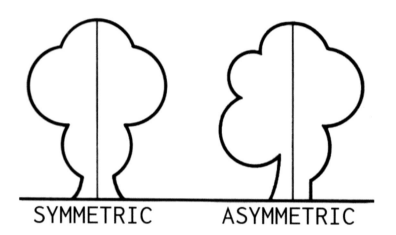

SYMMETRIC   ASYMMETRIC

In art, the picture on the left has formal balance. It is symmetrical. The picture on the right of the tree has informal balance. It is not symmetrical.

On the left is a picture of Celtic knotwork. Go to this website for more examples: http://www.thinkythings.org/knotwork/knotwork.html
Draw a Celtic knot from these website instructions.

Do you see the symmetry in this butterfly? Draw a butterfly and show symmetry in the wings.

28

Rotations:

Objectives:
- To understand the characteristics of the rotation of an object.
- To understand rotational symmetry.

As you might guess, rotations are moving the object or designs around a center point. For rotations you are looking for the angle you can rotate and get the same shape or image as you started with. We will look at a couple of designs to examine the rotations. You will need a protractor. Go to this website to see animated rotations: http://commons.wikimedia.org/wiki/Category:Animations_of_geometry

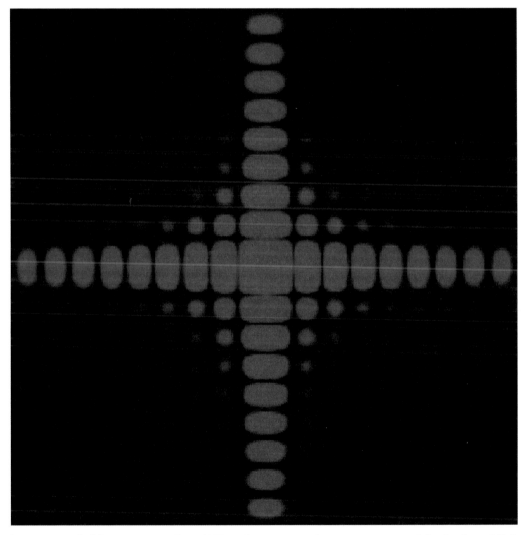

Rotating around this center point. What happens when you rotate this design 45 degrees? Does it look the same? 90 degrees? Although the length of the lights are different lengths, you do have the same pattern, and they would be the same if the photograph taken would have been square. Therefore, the design has rotational symmetry at 90 degrees. Rotational symmetry means the object looks the same. At what other two angles, other than 360 degrees, does this design have rotational symmetry? Go to this site see an animated rotation: http://simple.wikipedia.org/wiki/Image:Rotating_Sphere.gif

Line Designs

Objectives:
Making a design using straight lines and angles
Study right, acute and obtuse angles

For this project, you will need paper, pencil, protractor and compass. To make the design more colorful you may want to use colored paper and colored pencils.

To get your designs to work out well, you need to make accurate measurements and straight lines. For your first design, you will form a curve from straight lines:

1. Start with a right angle or 90 degrees.   2. Divide the sides into equal parts.   3. Connect the points.

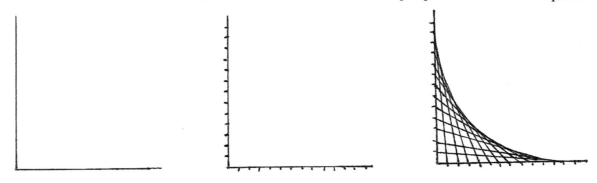

This is just one kind of design you can make. Things you can vary include:

1. Angle size: you may use an obtuse angle (greater than 90 degrees) or an acute angle (less than 90 degrees).

2. Spacing of your marks may be equal or unequal.

3. You could eliminate some spaces from the connections.

Let's try another one:

1. Start with an obtuse triangle. An obtuse triangle has an obtuse angle in it.   2. Divide the side into parts.   3. Connect the points

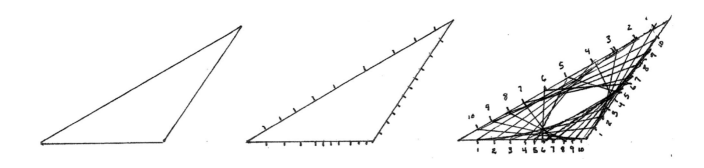

30

The picture above is of a string design.

Be Creative:

You may vary how you do this design to make string art. You need some kind of hard surface that will hold a small nail. You will need somewhere between a 6 to 9 inch square. You either need to cover your surface with fabric, or sand and stained wood. You will just need to ensure your background is attached to show your string. Then draw your angle or object on your background. Pick out string that will contrast with your board so it shows up. When you are dividing your object into spaces, you will place a small tack nail at those points. You will then use embroidery thread to connect the points, just like you connected the points with your pencil. For a wonderful animation of a curve go to: http://en.wikipedia.org/wiki/B%C3%A9zi er_curve#Quadratic_curves

Two-dimensional objects

Objectives: Explore properties of two-dimensional objects
Explore perimeters of two-dimensional objects
Explore area of two-dimensional objects

Two dimensional objects are exactly as they are named. They have two dimensions. They have length and width, but they are flat. We will examine some 2-dimensional objects and their characteristics, and the formula for their perimeter and area. **Perimeter** means the distance around the object. **Area** means the space inside the object.

Rectangle- All rectangles have 2 sets of parallel, opposite sides that are the same length. The angles are 90 degrees or right angles. To find the perimeter you would measure all the way around, which would be, L+W+L+W. When you simplify this it would be, P= 2L+2W. The area would be A=L x W.

Square-A special kind of rectangle is a square. What is special about a square? It has four equal sides. It has opposite sides that are parallel, and meet at a right angle, or 90 degrees. To find the perimeter of a square it would be side+side+side+side or P=4 sides
A=side x side 5 X 5 = 25   5 squared is 25
Here are the measurements for the square below: P=4 X 5   P=20   A=5 X 5   A=25

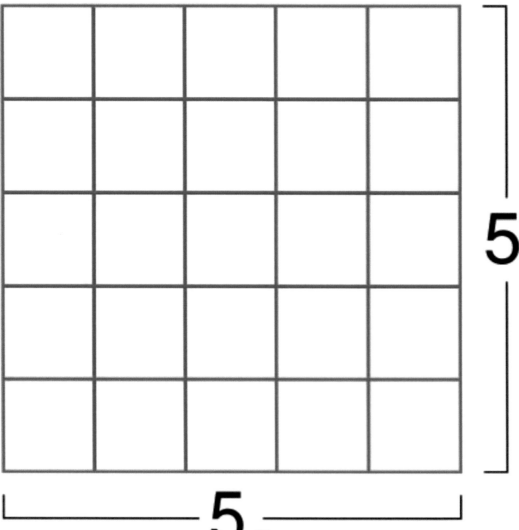

Compass

A tool used to draw a perfect circle is a compass. In the picture below from the 13th century, the compass was seen as a symbol of God's act of Creation. It was believed God created the universe after geometric and harmonic principles. Scholars felt to seek these principles was therefore to seek and worship God. Today, we don't believe this.

For a wonderful website on how to use a compass, go to:
http://www.makeitsolar.com/science-fair-ideas/90-find-circle-center.htm
Another wonderful site is:
http://www.princetonol.com/groups/iad/lessons/elem/linda-mandala.htm

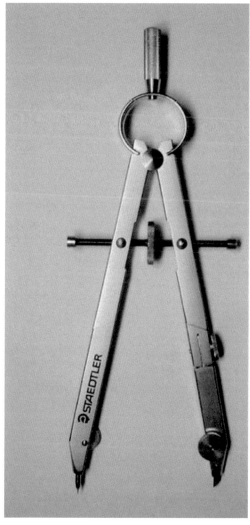

Circle

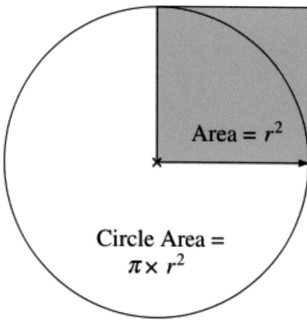

Area = r^2

Circle Area =
$\pi \times r^2$

To find perimeter or area of a circle a very special number and symbol needs to be used. It is pi, said pie. It is a number that goes on forever, so we often estimate it as 3.14. There are also a couple of terms we need to examine. They are related to each other, radius and diameter.

Radius- the radius is the distance from the center of the circle to a point on the circle.

Diameter- The distance from a point on the circle to the opposite side going through the center point. The diameter will be twice the measure of the radius.

Now, to find the perimeter of the circle, it will be pi times the diameter or pi times the diameter or pi d. Go to this excellent website: http://www.mathopenref.com/circumference.html To find the area, it will be pi times radius times radius or pi r2. Go to this website:http://www.mathgoodies.com/lessons/vol2/circle_area.html

Fill in the chart provided below with the characteristics of the shapes given, plus the formulas for perimeters and areas. Then draw an example of each one.

	CHARACTERISTICS	PERIMETER	AREA	DRAW OBJECT
RECTANGLE				
SQUARE				
TRIANGLE				
CIRCLE				

A triangle is a three-sided figure. The perimeter would be the distance around the triangle, or side +side+side. There are three kinds of triangles based on the length of their sides:

equilateral-all sides are equal

isoceles-two sides are equal

scalene-no sides are equal

Can you figure how finding perimeter would vary for each of these kinds of triangles?

Drawing them out may help.

To find the area of the triangle, you need to know the height.

The height is a line that is perpendicular (90 degrees) to the base, and meets at the point of the triangle. The formula is A=1/2 bh

Below are examples of how triangles may be catagorized according to their angles.

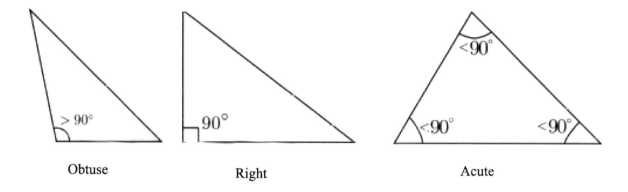

Obtuse   Right   Acute

Be Creative:

We can use the shapes we have been studying to make some interesting art. Make an abstract work of art out of an obtuse, right and 2 acute angles. Color it in red, yellow and blue, the primary colors.

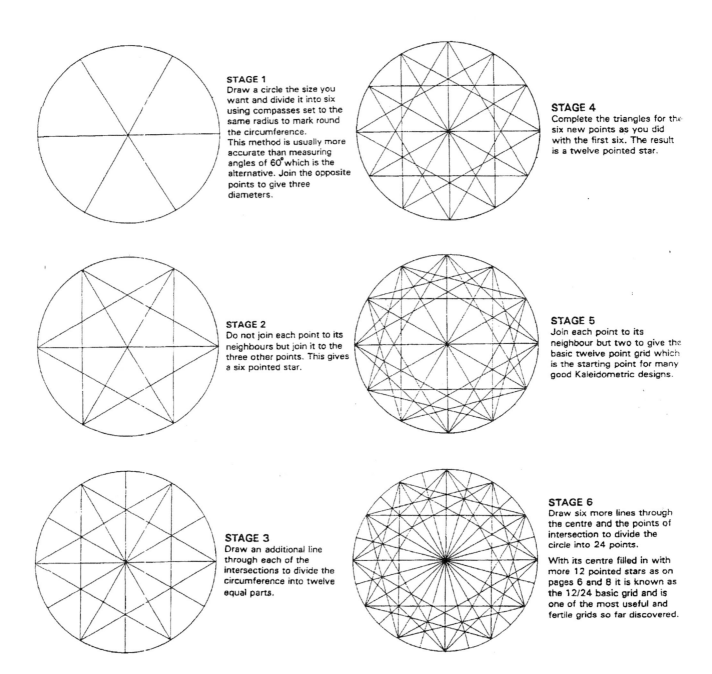

STAGE 1
Draw a circle the size you want and divide it into six using compasses set to the same radius to mark round the circumference.
This method is usually more accurate than measuring angles of 60° which is the alternative. Join the opposite points to give three diameters.

STAGE 2
Do not join each point to its neighbours but join it to the three other points. This gives a six pointed star.

STAGE 3
Draw an additional line through each of the intersections to divide the circumference into twelve equal parts.

STAGE 4
Complete the triangles for the six new points as you did with the first six. The result is a twelve pointed star.

STAGE 5
Join each point to its neighbour but two to give the basic twelve point grid which is the starting point for many good Kaleidometric designs.

STAGE 6
Draw six more lines through the centre and the points of intersection to divide the circle into 24 points.

With its centre filled in with more 12 pointed stars as on pages 6 and 8 it is known as the 12/24 basic grid and is one of the most useful and fertile grids so far discovered.

Be Creative:

Use the diagram above and make a kaleidoscope design. Go to this website and make your own Kaleidoscope: http://www.kaleidoscopesusa.com/makeAscope.htm.   Use complemetary colors to color the design. Use green beside red, orange beside blue, and yellow beside purple.   Complementary colors are colors across from each other on the colorwheel.

You can use basic shapes to design a quilt.
Let students use basic shapes and go to this website to see how to put them together:
http://www.freequiltpatterns.info/QuiltCategories/FreeBeginnerQuiltPatterns.htm

Use a compass to make your circles, and a ruler to make your straight lines. It adds spark if you overlap your shapes.
Make a collage: Choose brightly colored paper and print paper and cut these into basic shapes. Decide what the center of interest will be.

The picture on the left is of a hex sign. This is a Pennsylvania Dutch form of folk art. The star in the center is made from two triangles; one on top of the other.

37

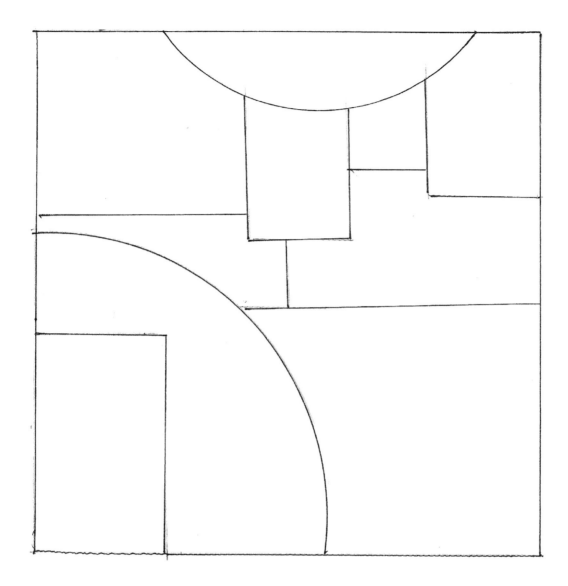

Be Creative:

Use markers or colored pencils and color the design above. You can go to this website to see a design by Mondrian, one of the most famous abstract artists in history. Mondrian began producing grid-based paintings in late 1919.   Go to this website to see "Composition in Yellow, Blue and Red"
http://en.wikipedia.org/wiki/Image:Mondrian_CompRYB.jpg
Make your own abstract design using red, yellow and blue. Red, yellow and blue are primary colors.

Be Creative:

For our first project you may refer to the illustration above. You will need a paper plate or heavy paper to glue objects to. Look around the house for three dimensional objects that you can find to glue onto your background. You may want to cover your objects with colored paper or wrapping paper. Or you could paint the objects different designs. Decide how you want your objects arranged on your background and glue or use a hot glue gun. You may want to also paint on your background to be more creative.

Make a three dimensional sculpture of your drawing. You will want something very heavy on the bottom to give stability. For the objects, cover them with paper to create a design. You can also use markers, paint or crayons and create designs. It will take several objects to complete your design. You will have a sculpture that is an example of modern decor. You might want to put the item in your room!

Fibonacci Sequence

Objectives:

What the Fibonacci Sequence looks like in nature

How to understand the sequence

One of the exciting things about mathmatics is how many things in nature work as a mathmatical formula. We have an incredibily designed world, as we will find out!

The Fibonacci Sequence is one of the mathematical sequences that appear in nature. It appears in the shape of a snail's shell or any other similar shape. It is as follow: 1, 1, 2, 3, 5, 8, 13, 21, 34, 55, 89...and so on into infinity. It goes on forever without end. Can you continue the sequence? What are you doing to continue the sequence?

Below is a picture of Australian sculptor Andrew Rogers's 50-ton stone and gold sculpture entitled Golden Ratio located in Jerusalem. The height of each stack of stones, beginning from either end and moving toward the center, is the beginning of the Fibonacci sequence: 1, 1, 2, 3, 5, 8.

Above is a picture of the spiral staircase in the St. Augustine lighthouse.

Notice these spiral staircases on this page. Can you see the Fibernacci Sequence? Practice drawing a snail's shell. Think of how this sequence will work. Shading makes the shell look three dimensional. When you shade, you need to think what direction the light is coming from. Where the light hits the snail, it is lighter. On the opposite side of the part where the lights hits, it is darker. Shading, shadow and texture make things look real. Can you see what might look like an eye in the picture on the left?
To see an animation of this go to:
http://www.mathematische-basteleien.de/spiral.htm

The spiral staircase above was done by the master artist Rembrandt. Do you think he needed any mathmatical skills to draw the staircase above? The picture of the window on the right is also by Rembrandt. Do you think he had to use perspective to get his pictures to have depth? Rembrandt was a Baroque artist. He painted after the Renaissance masters discovered the laws of perspective.

The Golden Mean:

Objective: Observe the mathmatical properties of the Golden Mean.
Design a composition using the Golden Mean and a pattern from nature.

Web Resources: http://en.wikipedia.org/wiki/Golden_ratio

The golden ratio is an irrational number, meaning it goes on to infinity. It never ends. The ration equals 1.61803395. What is very interesting about this number is that if you subtract one from this number you get 0.61803398. And, if you were to take the reciprocal of the ratio you would get the same number. By taking the reciprocal it means that you are putting the 1.61803398 in the denominator like this.

The Wikipedia says, "In mathematics and the arts, two quantities are in the golden ratio if the ratio between the sum of those quantities and the larger one is the same as the ratio between the larger one and the smaller. The golden ratio is approximately 1.6180339887.[1]

At least since the Renaissance, many artists and architects have proportioned their works to approximate the golden ratio—especially in the form of the golden rectangle, in which the ratio of the longer side to the shorter is the golden ratio—believing this proportion to be aesthetically pleasing. Mathematicians have studied the golden ratio because of its unique and interesting properties."

The Golden Ratio

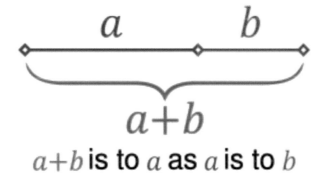

$a+b$ is to a as a is to b

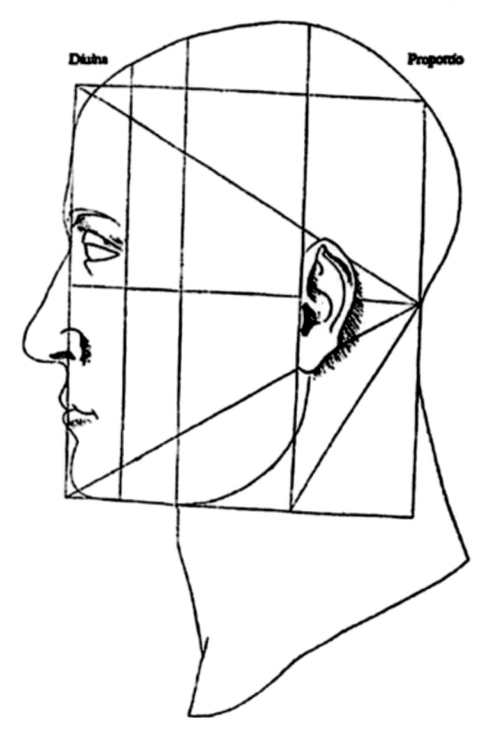

We saw the fractions in drawing a face correctly in a previous lesson. Here is the golden mean (rectangle) used by Leonardo da Vinci in drawing the face.

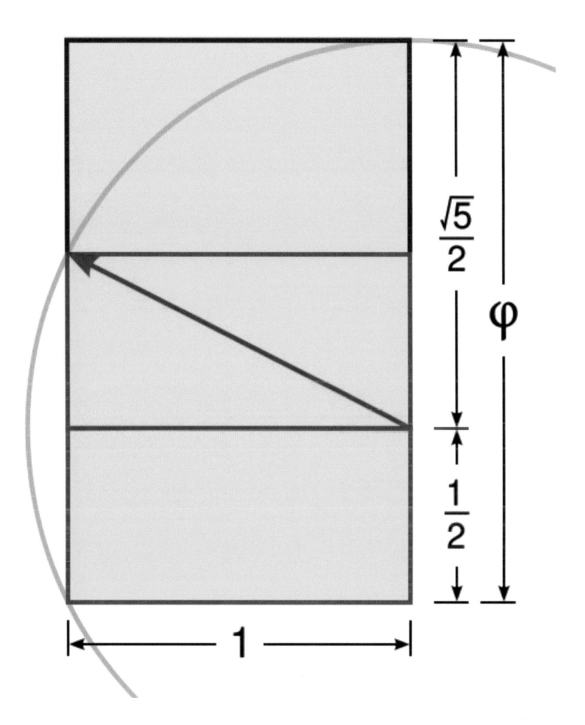

Golden Rectangle: Copy this drawing above and put every section of the rectangle in a different color of the colorwheel. Exclude the color red.

Parallel lines and One Point Perspective

Objectives:
Understand the properties of parallel lines
Discuss one point perspective
Parallel lines do not meet. They are the same distance apart as in the three illustrations below.

Go to page 49 for another explanation.

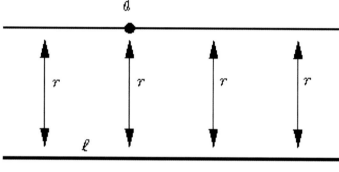

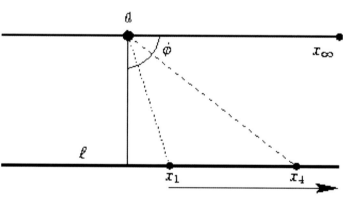

These are all examples of sets of parallel lines. The main thing to remember with parallel lines is they will stay the same distance from each other for the entire distance of the line, or line segment. When we draw in one or two point perspective using parallel lines, we create depth in a picture.
All vertical and horizontal lines will be parallel. Use the following page to learn about drawing with one point perspective. Pay attention to the parallel lines.

Notice in the picture below that the vertical and horizontal lines are parallel. The other lines meet at a vanishing point in the back of the painting. This is what creates depth in a picture. Shading will also create depth. Where is your light coming from in your picture? That area will be lighter, other areas will be darker. You can tell how large the door is by looking at how large the people are.

The above picture was done by Paola Ucello, Renaissance master artist and pioneer in the work of linear perspective. In the following pages, you will discover how math was used in his picture above. Can you try to copy the picture? Copy the picture again after your lessons on perspective are complete. Copy the picture and pay attention to the perspective.

1. Multiply the number of people on the left by 4. Draw that many boxes in the corner of the picture.

For one point perspective you choose a vanishing point. That is where all of your lines will meet. Notice the picture below. All of the lines intersect at the dot at the end of the walk way. Practice creating a drawing of your own using one point perspective. You need a ruler or some sort of straight edge.

1. Choose a vanishing point. This is the eye line.
2. Draw 7-8 lines coming out from the vanishing point. These need to be like the picture below or at similar angles.
3. Draw a box around a group of lines and do some erasing to create more of a drawing.
4. To create interest, you can add color. Hot colors are red, yellow and orange. Cool colors are blue, green and violet. Choose a color scheme to do your one point perspective in.

Law of one point perspective
All vertical lines are vertical, all horizontal lines are horizontal, all other lines meet at vanishing point.

If you were an architect, you might design the structure on the left. Each column is 8 feet tall. The distance between the columns in 8 feet. Can you estimate how long two parts of this structure might be? If someone asked you to design this arch for their garden, but you only had a 24 foot square space to do it in, what would be the dimensions? Draw a picture with the dimensions beside it.

One of the most famous paintings in history is a perfect one point perspective. "The Last Supper" by Leondardo da Vinci is a perfect example of one point perspective. Go to this web site for an excellent animated lesson: http://www.olejarz.com/arted/perspective/ showing one point perspective.

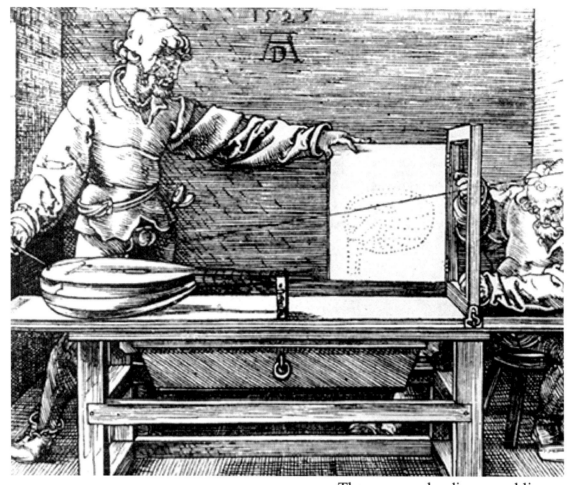

The person who discovered linear perspective was the artist and engineer, Brunelleschi. The first known perspective picture was made about 1415. Brunelleschi painted the Baptistery in Florence from the front gate of the unfinished cathedral. The picture is lost, but the painted panel was constructed with a hole at the vanishing point. The artist Dore in the picture above showed the procedure to get perspective to work. The picture was observed from the unpainted side and the reflection of the image was viewed in a mirror through the hole, giving the illusion of depth, thus perspective was born. When Brunelleschi designed pulleys to get the dome (that was in two pieces) in place on the left, he became the very first engineer!

Draw this room in a one-point perspective.

I find it easier to visualize what you are doing if you go ahead and draw a door, window, a picture or something on this end wall.

VP means vanishing point.

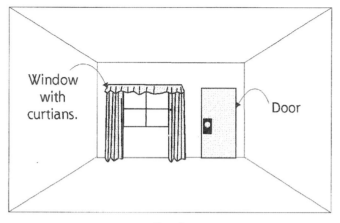

fig. 3

Construction lines from the VP Drawn very lightly.

Objects that are nearly flat, are easiest to add to the walls, floors and ceiling. Objects such as windows, rugs, pictures and lights. As these objects are added the room begins to become realistic (see fig. 4)

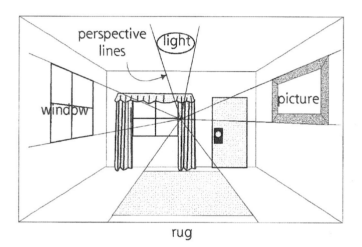

fig. 4

Construction lines are drawn lightly and erased to avoid confusion (see fig. 5)

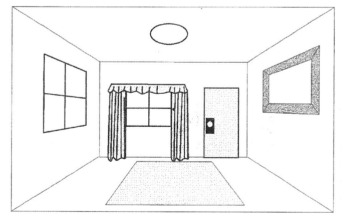

fig. 5

Be Creative:

Draw a room in your house. Use a ruler and put the vanishing point in the very center of wll furthest from you. Use this diagram and put as many details in the room as you can. Remember as you do this, all vertical lines are vertical, all horizontal lines are horizontal and all other lines meet at the vanishing point.

Do you remember from the last lesson on perspective we used one point perspective to show depth using parallel lines? Examine the photography on the left. Can you estimate where the vanishing point would be? Can you use a ruler and find the vanishing point?

Notice on the street, the parallel lines stay parallel lines. When they become smaller, this also shows depth.

Show your understanding of one-point perspective.

1. You will need pencil, paper and ruler.
2. Select your vanishing point. You need to make this toward the right or left edge of the paper.
3. Lightly draw all your lines to the vanishing point. This will give you your main lines.
4. Add vertical lines. Remember in a one point perspective, all vertical lines are vertical, all horizontal lines are horizontal, and all other lines meet at the vanishing point.
5. Darken all lines that need to be darkened and erase all lines that need to be erased.
6. Shade where needed to give your picture the appearance of depth; a three dimensional appearance.

The picture on the right is a table of perspective done in 1728.

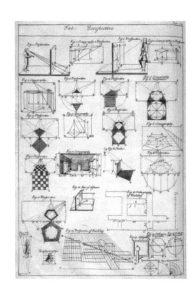

Three dimensional objects

Objectives:
Characteristics of 3 dimensional objects
Naming a variety of 3 dimensional objects
Understanding a cross section

In this lesson we are looking at objects that have three dimensions; length, width, and height. They are not flat. Just as two dimensional objects have length and width, three dimensional objects have length, width and heigth.

A rectangular prism is a 3 dimensional object that has a rectangle on all sides. It has width, length and height. If you want to find the volume, you multiply the dimensions. V=width x length x height

A rectangular prism has six sides. The top and the bottom are the same, the front and the back are the same, and the right and left are the same.

Surface area would be a matter of finding the area of each of the faces and multiplying by two.

A cube is a special kind of rectangular prism just like a square is a special kind of rectangle. For the cube width, length and height are all the same. So volume = side x side x side or "side cubed."

For surface area, all six sides are squares with an area of S squared or S = 6 s squared.

52

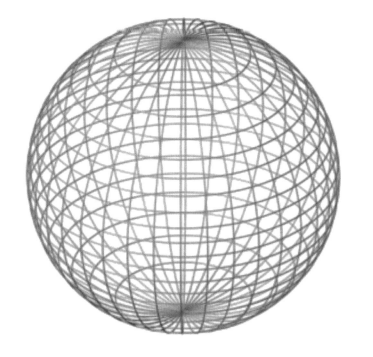

The second object is a sphere. If you cut through a sphere you will get a circle. That is the process of finding the cross section. Think of three spherical objects you use.

The third object is a cylinder. the cylinder has a circle for the top and the bottom. You can take two different cross-sections of this object. One is going across. If you cut it going up and down, you would get a rectangle. You could also cut it going across. What shape would you get? Name three objects you use that are a cylinder. Practice drawing a cylinder.

Make a list of all the things in the room you are in that are a sphere. Make a list of all the things that are a cylinder.

The image on the left is from Robert Webb's Great Stella software as the creator of this image along with a link to the Stella website: http://www.software3d.com/Stella.html.k

Be Creative:

Notice where the shading is in the cylinder above. The light comes from the above left corner. Use toilet paper rolls and paper towel rolls and anything you might throw away that is in the shape of a cylinder. Go to this website to see work by Nevelson who created assemblage art from throw away objects: http://en.wikipedia.org/wiki/Louise_Nevelson

This is an example of a cone. The base is a circle and it meets at a point perpendicular to the radius of the circle. It is called three dimensional because it has three dimensions; height, width and depth. Can you think of three examples of cones around you? Look at how the cone is shaded. Use shading on your cone. This will give the illusion of three dimensions. If you cut through a three dimensional object, you get a cross section.   If you make a horizontal cut through a cone, you get a circle. If you cut on a slanted level, you get an oval. Draw this cone and color from dark to light blue. Make sure it is darker on both sides so it looks three dimensional.

This mechanical robot made from basic three dimensional shapes you see below is from the Superman series. You can see one point perspective in the picture, too. Design a mechanical monster for a comic series. Use seven basic geometric solids: cone, sphere, cylinder, cube, rectangular prism, tetrahedron (pyramid), and octahedron.

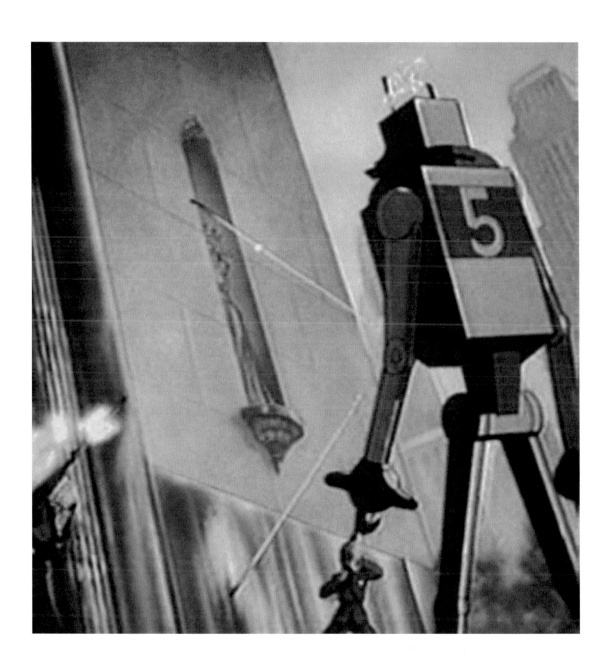

One of the most delightful projects I have done with students is a "Geometric bad hair day."

We talk about a bad hair day and I draw a face with the correct fractional proportions. They then try to put as many of the shapes below that they can into one picture. They can put a flower pot in the background or foreground; but I want them to show depth by putting a foreground and a background in the picture. Hair can be any color or texture, but it needs to look awful. The hair needs to look like "A Bad Hair Day."

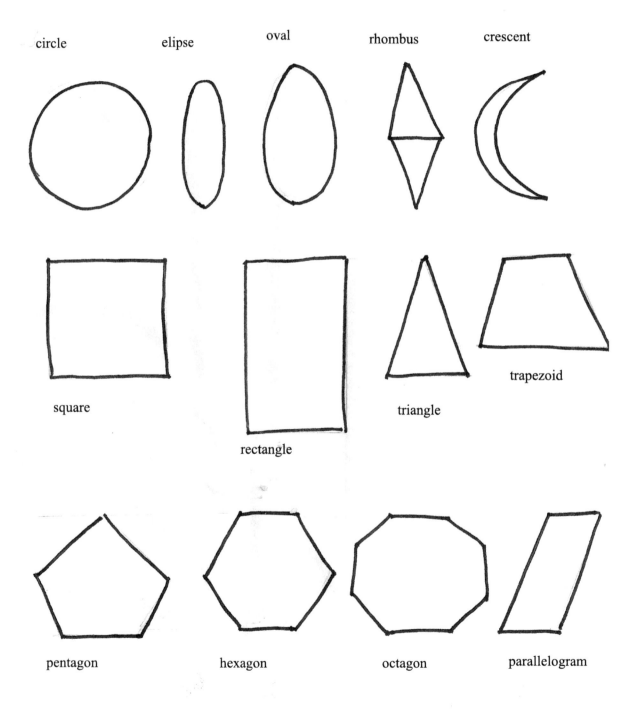

circle   elipse   oval   rhombus   crescent

square   rectangle   triangle   trapezoid

pentagon   hexagon   octagon   parallelogram

The picture above is a drawing of Frank Stella's "The Science of Laziness." Do
your own abstract design and then give it a name. Go to this website to see "Three
Musicians" by Picasso. Does it look anything like the title?
http://www.thepianoschool.net/images/three_musicians_moma.jpgj

Assessment: Label the geometric shapes above. Draw the shapes below and shade them similar to the drawing above. Make your own drawing of five shapes. Shade them to look three-dimensional.

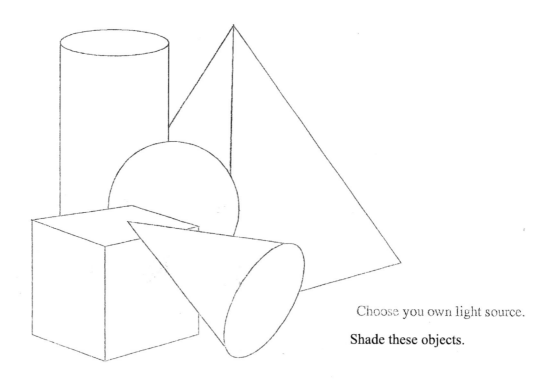

Choose you own light source.

Shade these objects.

Whoever makes a DESIGN, without the Knowledge of PERSPECTIVE,
will be liable to such Absurdities as are shewn in this Frontispiece.

The above picture is a "Satire on False Perspective" by Hogarth. Circle parts of the picture that are not in correct perspective. After you read about two point perspective, draw a picture where you purposely do everything that is not in correct perspective similar to what Hogarth did above.

Two point perspective:

On the line provided below draw a box in perspective. If you need to, refer to the drawing of the box in fig. 3, for help.

Figure 3 is on next page.

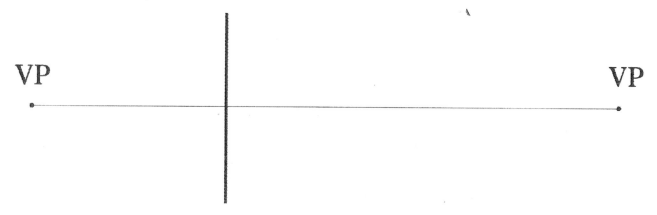

Now draw a box in perspective below the line provided. If you need to, refer to the drawing of the box in fig. 6, for help.

Figure 6 is on next page.

If you want to see what a box that is above the horizon line looks like, turn this page upside down.

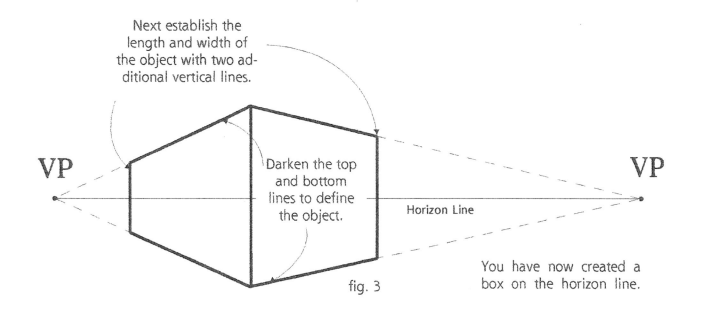

Next establish the length and width of the object with two additional vertical lines.

VP

Darken the top and bottom lines to define the object.

Horizon Line

VP

fig. 3

You have now created a box on the horizon line.

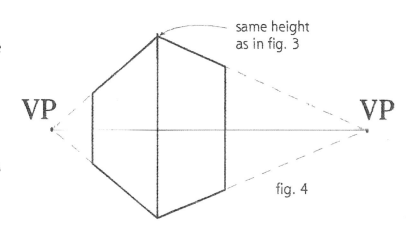

You should notice that if you move the vanishing points farther apart or closer together you can change the perspective dramatically.

Fig.4 has a shorten horizon line with the same height and fig.5 has an elongated horizon line with the VP off of the page.

same height as in fig. 3

VP

VP

fig. 4

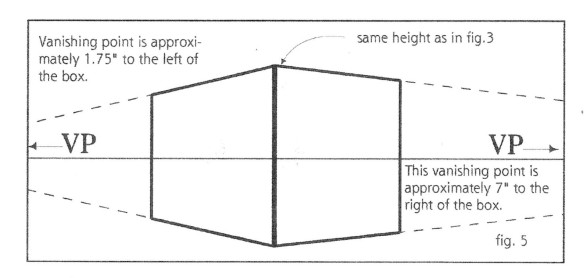

Vanishing point is approximately 1.75" to the left of the box.

same height as in fig.3

VP

VP

This vanishing point is approximately 7" to the right of the box.

fig. 5

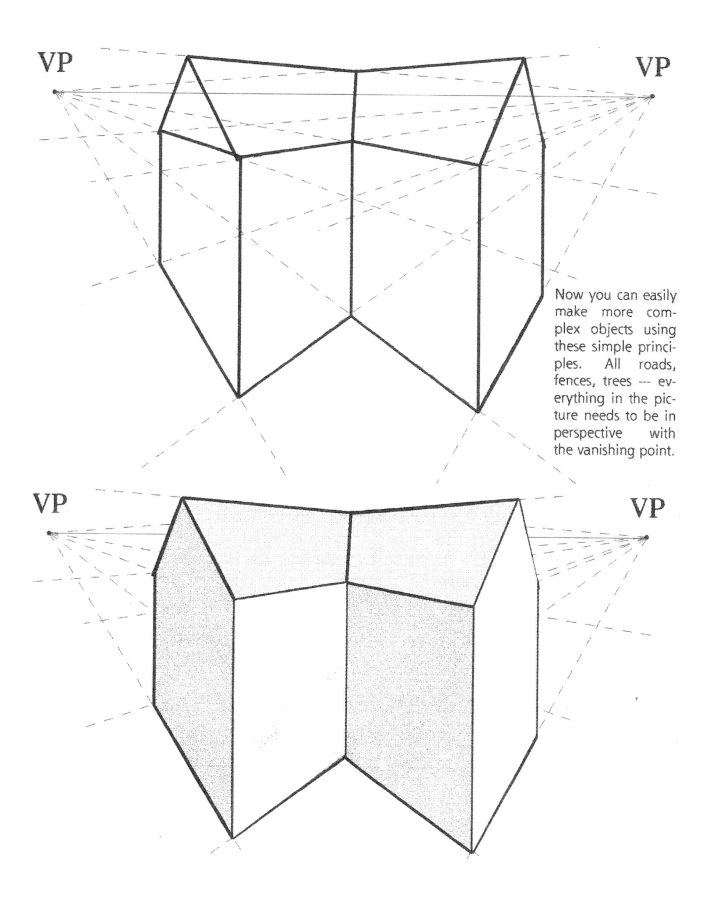

VP

VP

Now you can easily make more complex objects using these simple principles. All roads, fences, trees --- everything in the picture needs to be in perspective with the vanishing point.

VP

VP

Working with Color:
Objectives:
-Understanding color.
-Using paints to create color
-Proportions effect mixing color.

We will start out by looking at some theories about color. In mathematics a theory is used to refer to distinct bodies of knowledge about mathematics. This knowledge includes definitions, theories and computational techniquest, all related in some way by tradition or practice.

Many historical "color theorists" have believed that three "pure" primary colors can mix all possible colors. These three colors are blue, red and yellow. When mixed in equal parts, they produce the secondary colors. Blue mixes with yellow to produce green; red and yellow are orange; and blue and red are violet. Thus, green, orange, and violet are the secondary colors. You may also affect the hue of any color by adding white. Doing this creates a lighter shade, or a pastel. For instance, when you add white to red, you will get pink.

Warm vs. Cool Colors

The distinction between warm and cool colors has been important since at least the late 18th Century. The contrast seems to relate to the observed contrast in the "cool" landscape light versus the "warm" colors associated with daylight or sunset. Warm colors are often said to be hues from red through yellow, browns and tans included. Cool colors include hues from blue-green through blue-violet, with most grays included. Warm colors are said to appear most active in a painting, while cool colors tend to be calm and quiet. When in interior design or fashion, warm colors are said to arouse or stimulate, cool colors calm and relax.

Even when you do have the same color, you have a multitude of differing hues of that color. Imagine, your eyes and brain are processing all of those colors all at the same time, even the smallest detail. Something else to think about, do you like watching TV or video games? Your eyes and brain are at work absorbing all that color and movement continually. Our brain and senses are certainly the most amazingly made computer ever!

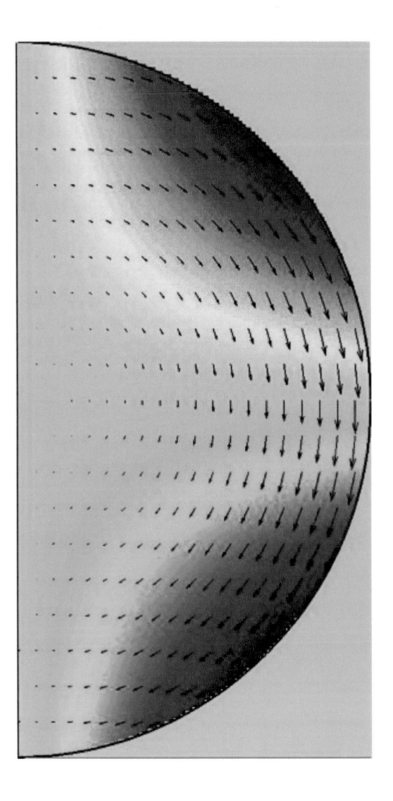

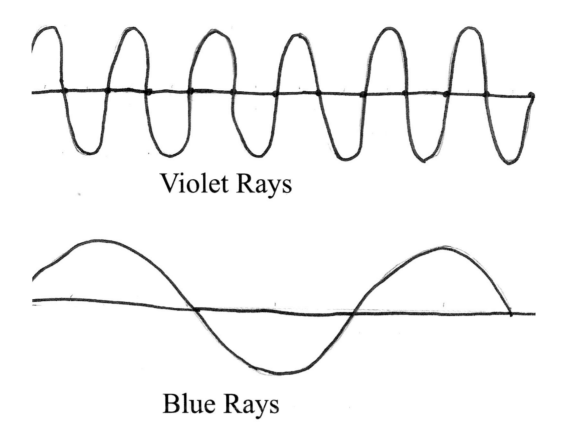

Violet Rays

Blue Rays

Copy the picture above, however, make the ray lines very thick. Turn them into the colors of the colorwheel in correct order. Attempt to make the lines look like the colors flow one color into another.

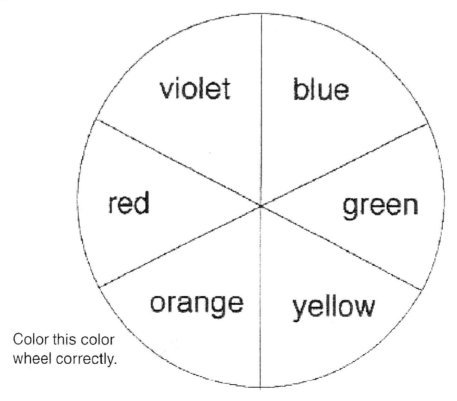

violet | blue

red | green

orange | yellow

Color this color wheel correctly.

How to use a ruler: A ruler is an instrument used in geometry, technical drawing and engineering/building and art to measure distances and/or to draw straight lines. A ruler is a foot. You can measure it this way....1 Inch = 2.54 cm, 1 Feet = 30.48 cm, 1 Feet = 12 Inch. Use your ruler and measure the cups and glasses in your kitchen.

Drawing with Grids

Part 1

When wanting to get a more exact replication of another picture, or to make your own drawing a larger or smaller size, you draw even squares (a grid) all over the picture you want to copy, and then put corresponding squares on your paper. One of the easiest ways to do this is to use a 12 inch ruler and trace the ruler all the way across the paper you will be drawing on. Then take the picture you are copying and put the same grid size grid on it. This will help you to focus on the details and proportions of the picture you are copying. If you want to make the picture larger, you can make larger squares on your drawing paper. All that is important is that all squares are perfectly even. Use your ruler to measure this.

This is a good project in learning to measure and use a ruler, but very encouraging to the new artist in results!

Objective:

Understanding anamorphic pictures

Demonstrate grid distortion

The underlying idea of transforming information from one grid to another has a long histroy in both mathmatics and art. When the blank grid differs from the original grid, the drawing can suffer intriguing distortions. In art, the result is something called an anamorphic picture. Mathmatically you are looking at the results of a type of transformation or mapping.

Creating a transformation:

1. Choose a picture to distort. Don't pick a picture that is too small.
2. Draw a grid on the picture. The size of the grid depends on the size of your picture.
3. You now begin with drawing your grid for your transformation. Begin with the same height as your original grid.
4. Divide the height in half. To the right draw the vanishing point. Then divide the height equally into the same number of parts as the original grid. Draw each of these to the vanishing point. Be sure these lines are equal in distance.
5. Now you need to put in your vertical lines. Again, you need the same number parts as your original grid. To create perspective, you should place the vertical lines closer together as you get further away.
6. When you complete your grid, you should have the same number of trapezoids as squares from the grid.
7. You are now ready to transform your picture to the new grid. Your method of grid transformation is the same as in the original lesson, only your new image will appear distorted.

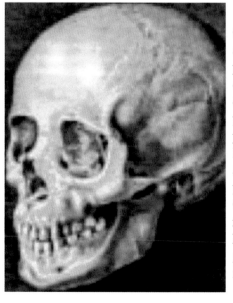

Can you take the picture and morph a grid to get this picture? If you wanted to do yet another type of distortion, when you make your grid to transfer your picture, you could use wavy lines. This is a challenging assignment but would give you an interesting picture. Go to these websites for more wonderful lessons: http://www.princetonal.com/groups/iad/lessons/middle/grid-drawings.htm

Author, Angie Gray did the praying hands below using the grid method. Use the next two pages and draw the Praying Hands, by Durer. Duplicate the picture in as much detail as you can.

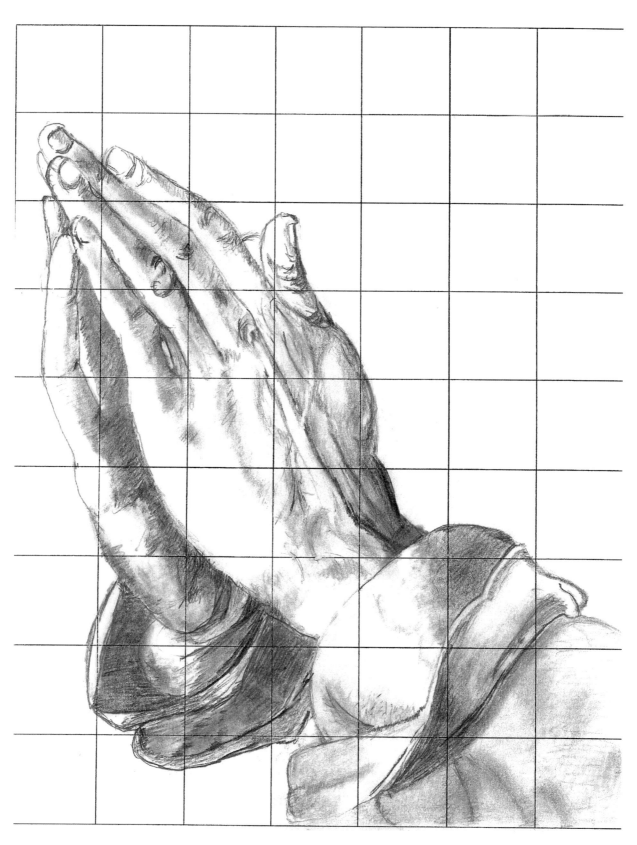

Albrect Durer did this picture of the hands of his brother in the 1500's. The story is that his brother sacrificed and worked so the Albrecht could go to art school. Look at what is in one square at a time and try to duplicate what is in that one square on the blank grid.

69

The figure in the foreground is really a skull that has been stretched or morphed. According to the Wikipedia, "The most notable and famous of Holbein's symbols in the work, however, is the skewed skull which is placed in the bottom centre of the composition. The skull, rendered in anamorphic perspective, another invention of the Early Renaissance, is meant to be nearly subliminal as the viewer must approach the painting nearly from the side to see the form morph into a completely accurate rendering of a human skull."

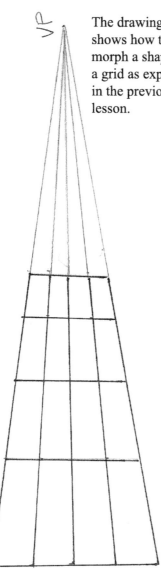

The drawing below shows how to morph a shape using a grid as explained in the previous lesson.

Fractals:

Go to this website to see an animated building of a fractal:http://en.wikipedia.org/wiki/Image:Von_Koch_curve.gif
http://en.wikipedia.org/wiki/Image:Animated_construction_of_Sierpinski_Triangle.gif
Go to this website to see how to build a Koch snowflake:
http://en.wikipedia.org/wiki/Image:Von_Koch_curve.gif
Go to this website to see the animated construction of a mountain:
http://en.wikipedia.org/wiki/Image:Animated_fractal_mountain.gif
Go to this website for an animated fractal:
http://en.wikipedia.org/wiki/Image:Phoenix%28Julia%29.gif

Fractals and Fractal Art

By Jonathan Jeffus

Many people could never imagine the possiblility of mathmatics and art sharing any common ground. In fact I think it's safe to say that most would call the relationship of math and art as a sort of uncomfortable suspicion. Many people major in art as a way to avoid math classes and every mathmatician I've met (and brought up the subject) considered themselves incapable of even basic drawing. It's a frequent dichotomy and it seems to not only be limited to the visual arts. Yet, I don't believe this should really be the case. Both mathmatics and art are founded on the creative solution of problems. The artist or writer has an ultimate goal and he must reach that goal by solving a series of problems, by following a set of rules. An artist must apply paint or mold clay following complex rules of perspective, shading, shadow and texture.

But more than that, the artist is primarily concerned with the creation of beauty, regardless what its form may take in their mind and ultimately their canvas. The American Heritage Dictionary defines beauty as "The quality that gives pleasure to the mind or senses and is associated with such properties as harmony of form or color, excellence of artistry, truthfulness, and originality."

Here we find the true linking of art and mathmatics. In many of the great equations of science you will find qualities that after you think about them a bit, you will realize that they represent the most pure harmony of form, the highest order of excellence, an irrefutable truthfulness and profound originality. All the earmarks of beauty.

I'm going to show you one of these equations. It's really short and there'll be no tedius algebra homework assigned afterward. In fact you probably have seen this before. It comes from a man who lived in Cretona, Greece over 2,500 years ago by the name of Pythagorus. $a^2 + b^2 = c^2$.

One kind of art that closely relates to math is fractal art. What is fractal art and what is a fractal? Well, a fractal is a geometric pattern that is rough and fragmented. Fractals were given their name in 1975 when Benoit Mandelbrot published his book A Theory of Fractal Sets after 20 years of research. A line is one dimensional and a plane is two dimesional, yet if a line curves in such a way as to cover the entire surface of a plane then it becomes something that is not quite two dimensional and not quite one dimensional (actually this kind of thing occurs between the 2nd, 3rd and 4th dimensions as well.

Mandelbrot described it as a fractional dimension between one and two dimensions. The most famous fractal set is named after Mandelbrot and is thus called the $x_{n+1} = x_n^2 + c$.

When the results of this equation are plotted (with z and c as complex numbers) we get the Mandelbrot set.

73

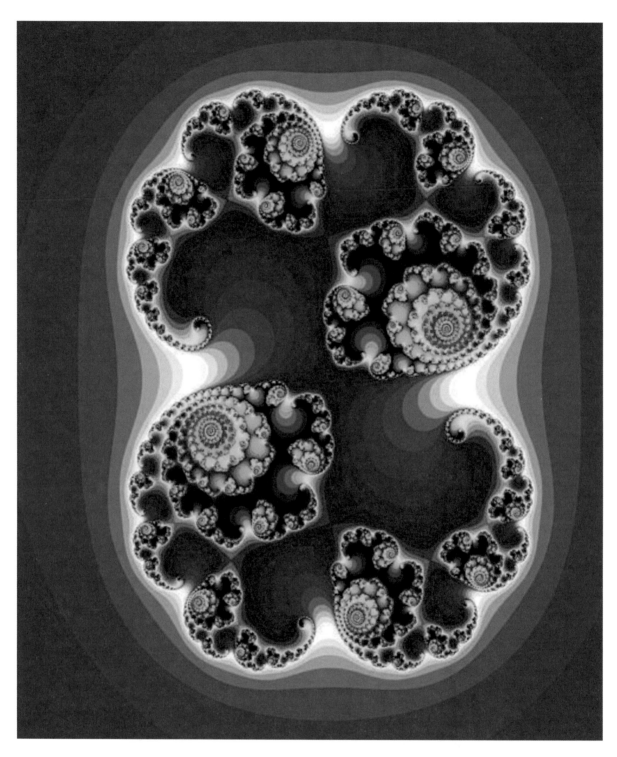

The above fractal is called a Julia set. According to the Wikipedia, a fractal is considered "a rough or fragmented geometric shape that can be subdivided into parts, each of which is (at least approximately) a reduced-size copy of the whole,"[1] a property called self-similarity. Can you see the similarities in the geometric shapes? Can you see similarities in intensity? Go to this website to see it in color:

http://commons.wikimedia.org/wiki/Image:Julia_set_%28highres_01%29.jpg

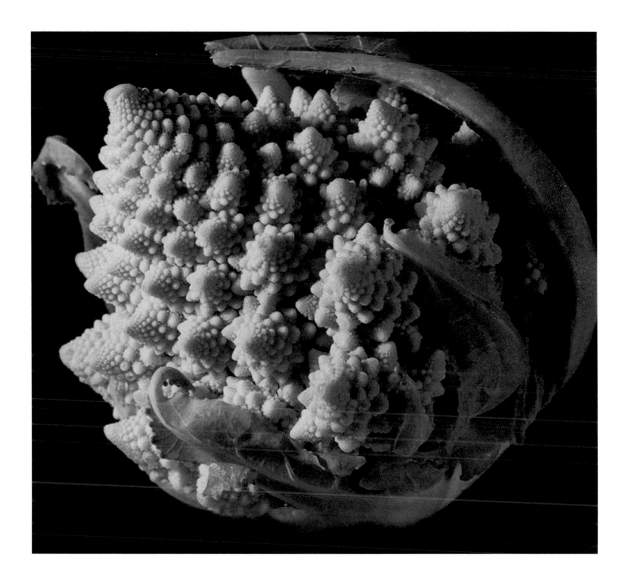

Be Creative:

Broccoli is actually a fractal. Use a piece of black paper to draw the picture above. Use shades of green and white. Can you replicate the picture above? The black is negative space, the broccoli is the positive space. Do you think someone could recognize it if you didn't tell them what it was? Look at the fractal on the right. Can you recognize any specific things in the fractal? I see something that looks like feet.

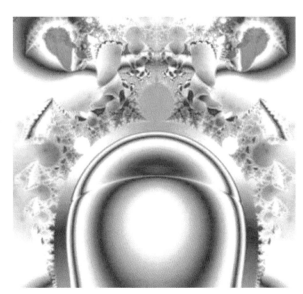

Make the shape on this
page half as large as it is.
Color it in only two colors
of the colorwheel.

Metamorphosis picture:

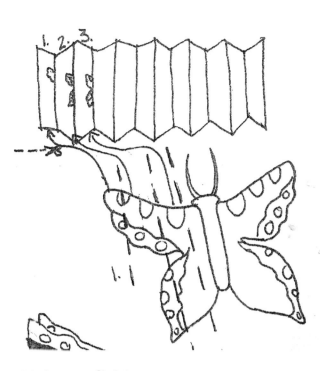

Take 2 pieces of regular size copy paper. Do a picture of caterpillar on one of the sheets, filling up the paper and using bright colors. Do a picture of a butterfly on the other sheet using bright colors and filling up the paper. Measure strips one inch by one inch on each sheet of paper. Number these strips and cut them out. Take a sheet of 12" by 18" paper and fold it into one inch strips. Alternately glue the two pictures on the large folded paper. It will be a fan shape. When you look from one side it will be a butterfly. When you look from the other side, it will be a caterpillar. When you look from the front it will be an abstract.

Using a Grid

Below is an architectural drawing. Notice the paper is a grid. Math is used in measurement by architects. Draw a floor plan for a building you would like to design. Use grid paper.

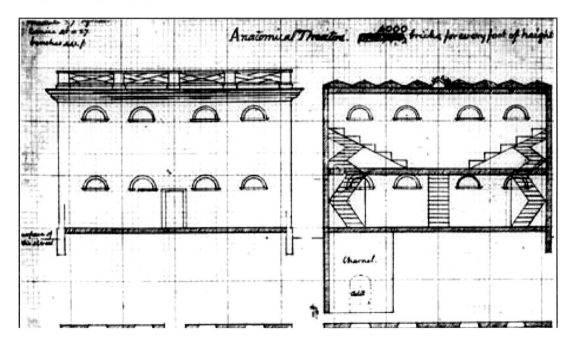

Weaving is very mathmatical and symmetrical. The two weavings on the following pages are from North Africa. Copy these weavings using small grided paper. Now design your own woven rug. Make sure your design is symmetrical.

Copy this design on very small grid paper.

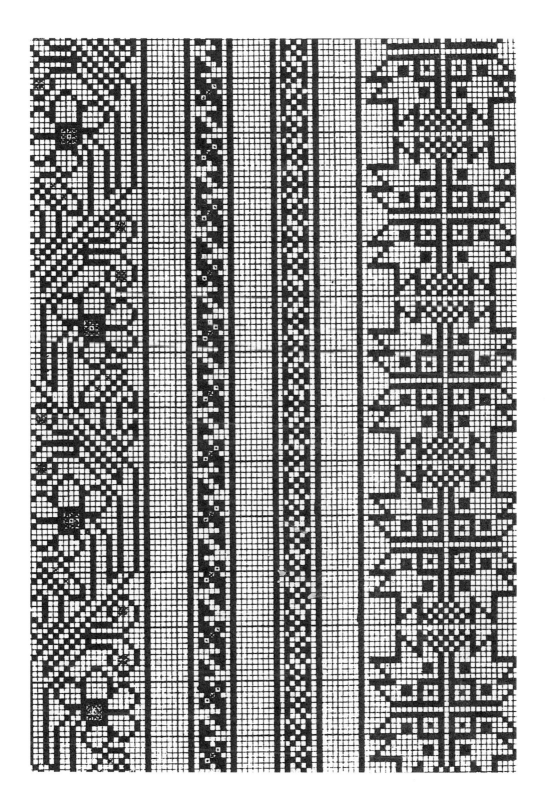

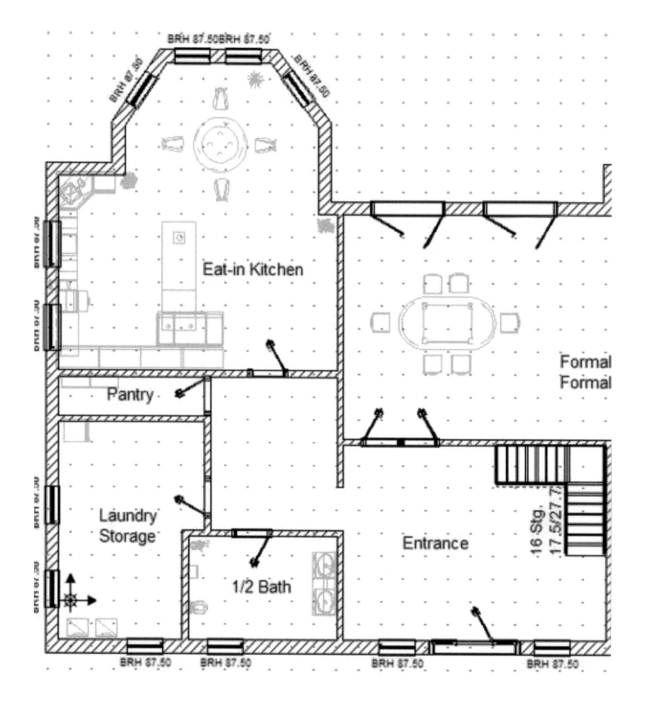

Be Creative:

When designing a house, you need to use a lot of math. Notice above you see the size of the rooms. Draw a house floor plan. The house will be 3000 square feet. Calculate how large each room will be. There are no lines in the grid used above. Do you see how the architect was able to get a balanced and measured design?

The people you are designing the house for want you to add another 500 feet to the living room. Redesign the house to suit your clients. I knew an architect in Arkansas who designed his house using the rock on the side of a mountain for an inner wall. Be creative.

The work of art above is called "Intrinsic Harmony," by Richard Anuszkiewicz, 1965. It is an abstract work of art. Abstract art does not represent anything real, it uses shapes and designs to create a picture. There are many angles used in this work of art. Design your own work of art using angles made with a protractor to fit a pattern. This work of art is done in red and blue and shades of red and blue. Do your design with the same color scheme.

Estimation:

The official definition of estimation according to the wikipedia is:
Estimation is the calculated approximation of a result which is usable even if input data may be incomplete and uncertain.
You need to be able to estimate numbers on a daily basis. If you are having a party, you need to estimate the amount of food you might need. How many people will be coming and how much will they eat? If you are going on a trip, you need to estimate how much money you will need to bring for gas. You need to estimate the amount of time you might njeed to complete a project.

An adult male walrus can weigh up to 4,500 pounds. Estimate how many pounds are seen in the picture below. Scientists does this by measuring the picture into parts. They count the number of walruses in that section and then multiply by the number of parts. Find a variety of pictures of groups of animals on the internet:
http://reference.aol.com/planet-earth/animals/animal-groups and then estimate their numbers.

Be Creative:

Our objective is to create a visual image showing measurements. A gallon has 4 quarts. A quart has two pints. A pint has 32 tablespoons. A tablespoon has 3 teaspoons. Create a creature that shows these measurements. Create a measurement jellyfish.
 Can you think of a creature that shows all the measurements visually?
 Where does the cup fit in?

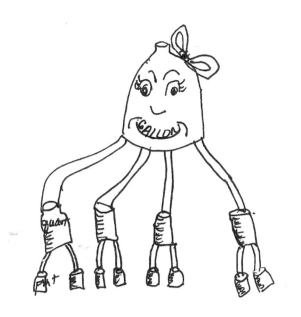

Measuring Horses by Hands:

A hand is a unit of length measurement. It is based on the breadth of a male human hand and now standardized at 4 inches.
Today the Hand is primarily used to describe the height of horses, ponies. You may have a horse that is 15 hands tall. This would be 60 inches tall.
 Can you estimate how tall a horse is just by looking at him? This measurement is used officially in different countries, including the USA, Australia, and the UK. In this context, one hand equals four inches (10.16 cm), and the horse is measured from the ground to the top of the withers.

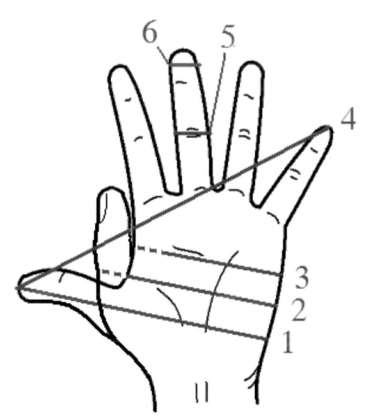

Measure a square that is 12 inches by 12 inches. You can fold this square into nine different parts just like the one below. If you cut on the dotted lines, you fold one end part of the three part squares up and one part down and fold the rest under for a chair shape. When you cut the same size square and fold it into twelve pieces, you get a couch shape. You just cut on the dotted lines. You can roll paper, add tissue paper and even stuff the tissue paper with cotten to get a pillow effect. Decorate your chair the way you think it would look best. I let my students design a throne for the Narnia movies. They love it.

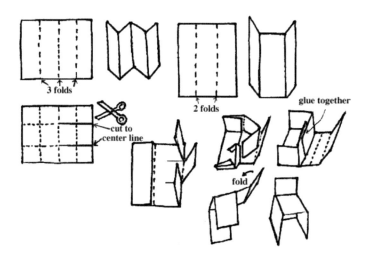

The pictures on the right and left are done by artists. The one on the left is the throne of Soloman. These are just two dimensional works of art. Work on adding details to your throne to turn it into a three dimensional work of art.

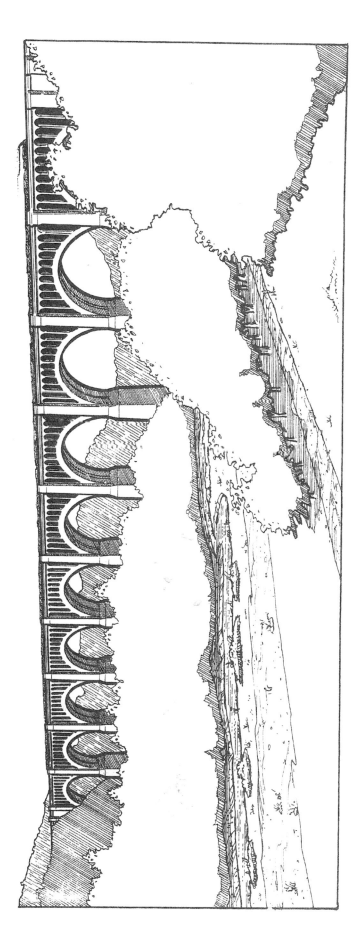

This is the Tunkhannock Creek Railroad Bridge in Pennsylvania.
It is 2, 375 feet from one end to the other. Estimate the distance between the arches.

Above is a picture of a bar of gold. The value is $10,000. How much would 12 of these be worth? If the cost of gold went down 10 %, how much would the same bars be worth? If the price of gold is dropping 5% a month, how much will it be worth in four months?

Design a chair. Be sure and give the heighth, width and length of the chair.   Make the chair 1/8 the size for your protype.

Solid oak Morris chair with adjustable back and loose cushioned seat. *Sears Catalog*

Nineteenth century mahogany parlor chair in the Roman style. *Sears Catalog*

Solid oak dining room chair with spindle back and carved top rail. *Montgomery Ward Catalog*

Nineteenth century wicker rocking chair. *Montgomery Ward Catalog*

Nineteenth century reed rocker with braided border. *Montgomery Ward Catalog*

Mahogany side chair with upholstered seat and shield back. *Furniture of Our Forefathers*

Hardwood dining chair with spindle back and pierced top rail. *Montgomery Ward Catalog*

Ornamental lady's reed rocker. *Montgomery Ward Catalog*

Gentleman's large reed rocking chair.

Hardwood dining

Draw and color the gumball machines on the left. Estimate how many gumballs are in one machine. Make one of the gumball machines half full. Make one one fourth full. Estimate how many gum balls might be in each one.

The length of this bridge is 13,700 feet. Estimate the height of the vertical columns. Also estimate the length of the boat below the bridge. When an engineer designs a bridge, he uses math in measuring the bridge.

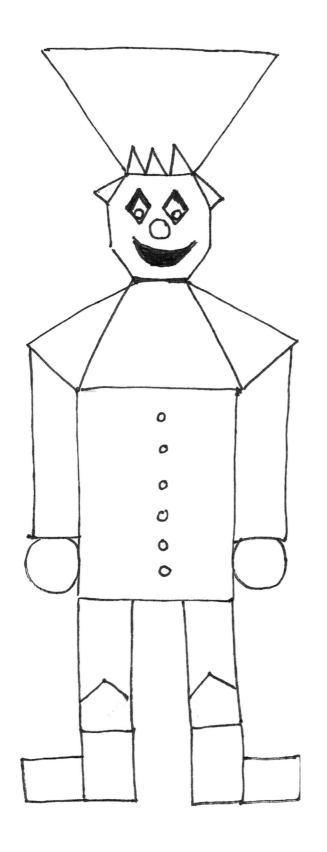

Be Creative:

You design the test. Use as many basic shapes as you can. Have each shape a certain dimension. Show reflection, rotation and symmetry in the finished picture. Send your picture to us and we will try to put it up in our art gallery. For more books by Visual Manna, go to visualmanna.com and check out our free lessons in art reinforcing core subjects. Email us at

visualmanna@gmail.com or snail mail us at Visual Manna P.O Box 494 Raymore, MO 64083 If you liked this book, go to visualmanna.com! We teach on the internet, too.

Art Camp in Kansas City the first week in June.

We would like to credit the following sources of images:
Borderbound Click Art
Sharon Jeffus
Richard Jeffus
Angie Gray
Dover Pictorial Archives

MORE BOOKS FROM VISUAL MANNA

Art Through the Core series...
  Teaching American History Through Art
  Teaching Astronomy Through Art
  Teaching English Through Art
  Teaching History Through Art
  Teaching Literature Through Art
  Teaching Math Through Art
  Teaching Science Through Art
  Teaching Social Studies Through Art

Other Books...
  Art Adventures in Narnia
  Art Basics for Children
  Bible Arts & Crafts
  Christian Holiday Arts & Crafts
  Dragons, Dinosaurs, Castles and Knights
  Drawing, Painting and Sculpting Horses
  Expanding Your Horizons Through Words
  Indians In Art
  Master Drawing
  Preschool & Early Elementary Art Basics
  Preschool Bible Lessons
  Visual Manna 1: Complete Art Curriculum
  Visual Manna 2: Advanced Techniques

Books available at Rainbow Resource Center:
www.rainbowresource.com • 888.841.3456

VISUAL | | MANNA

Educating with art since 1992!

A Christian is one whose imagination should fly beyond the stars. Francis Schaeffer

HIS LIONS

Contact *visualmanna@gmail.com* if you are interested in our Intern program. Students learn how to teach art, do murals for ministry, prepare an excellent portfolio, and much more. Go to **visualmanna.com** for information.

Free art lessons are available at **OurHomeschoolForum.com** and books are available at Rainbow Resource Center (**www.rainbowresource.com**). Try all our "Art Through the Core" series and other books as well! Make learning fun for kids!!! Sharon Jeffus teaches Art Intensives in person for the Landry Academy at **landryacademy.com**.

Made in the USA
Middletown, DE
26 April 2022